CROSSROADS
God's Road Map for Entrepreneurs
15 Marks of the Kingdom Blueprint

Audrea V. Heard

Published by I.B.G. Publications, LLC a Power to Wealth Company

Web Address: WWW.IBGPublications.Com

IBGPublications@Gmail.Com / 904-419-9810

This book or its parts may not be reproduced in any form, stored in a retrieval system, or transmitted in any form, by any means-electronic, mechanical, photocopy, recording or otherwise, without prior written permission of the publisher or author, except as provided by the United States of America Copyright law.

This book is intended to give sound advice about the business experiences of Audrea V. Heard, with wisdom divinely given by the Holy Spirit. This book's intention is to help business owners and marketplace ministers do business the way God intended and find His special design for their journey.

Unless otherwise noted, all scriptural references are taken from the King James Version of the Bible, unless otherwise noted.

Cover Design by IBG Publications.

Copyright 2020

DEDICATION

This book is dedicated to Entrepreneurs from all walks of life.

As you embark into the wonderful world of business, it is my hope and desire that you will allow God to be your source and guide. But most of all through your journey, allow Him to be your trusted confidant when no one else can see or understand your process.

You were on His mind when you obeyed His word and wrote the vision: ***Habakkuk 2:2.***

TABLE OF CONTENTS

DEDICATION
ACKNOWLEDGEMENTS
INTRODUCTION

Stick to the Blueprint!.................................	5
The Right Equipment......................	27
Flowing Streams...........................	39
A Solid Plan...............................	49
Submission to the Process...............	61
The Final Destination.....................	73
About Audrea V. Heard..................	81

ACKNOWLEDGMENTS

I acknowledge my Father, God, who is my continual inspiration for every book I write. Once again, He has given me words of hope and inspiration for someone else to live by.

I acknowledge the immediate members of the Heard Clan, who are all Entrepreneurs in their own right:
Walter T. Heard, III, still defining his own Entrepreneurial path. I believe God to release insight to you through this book.
Edward J. Heard, Owner of Second Shots Photography. Keep capturing those award winning shots!
Deseree A. Heard, owner of Alexandria's Angels: Continue showering a Mother's love on the children entrusted in your care. Your tender touch means more than you know!

Introduction

This book is inspired by my Entrepreneurial journey. Since 2002, I have been striving to be a full time, self-sufficient Entrepreneur. This was when I originally wrote the vision for my company: Power to Wealth Enterprises.

But little did I know the twists and turns my journey would take and the many crossroads which would juncture in my ongoing quest for success!

I can never forget when I received the first glance at my vision for business. I was working as a Cashier for Publix Grocers when the name, "Power to Wealth Enterprises" came to my spirit.

I was so excited, and I knew from the very beginning this was a vision that was larger than I was. This vision was larger than where I was standing in that cashiering line, on my feet for the entire shift!

In much anticipation, I went home and the Lord instructed me to go the scriptures. He took me directly to ***Deuteronomy 8:18***, which says:

"But remember the LORD *your God, for it is He who gives you the ability to produce wealth, and so confirms His covenant, which He swore to your ancestors, as it is today."*

What a huge promise God made to me that day! Not only was this a promise He made to Moses, but

He was reiterating this promise to me also. He was granting this promise to me on a scale much larger than anything I had ever dreamed or imagined.

In order to fully understand this promise, let's take a closer look at what God was telling Moses.

Moses' Track Record...

Don't forget the history of Moses and the Children of Israel. Don't forget all of the trials they endured and how they continued to wander around in the wilderness for the span of 40 years.

But this did not disqualify them from the promise!

God wanted them to understand that the *POWER* to obtain wealth *only* comes from Him. It did not come from the people or place He was sending them, no matter how much they were *told* it was flowing with milk and honey.

It is and always has been God's intention to grant His children wealth. No matter how long the children of Israel ran around in the wilderness, disobeyed God, and at times walked contrary to His laws, His desire was to bless them with wealth and increase.

Here in His word, God was revealing a secret to them. The secret was: The Power was already within them and within their hands to obtain the wealth He promised!

When we advance further into the scriptures, we

can determine that when God sent Joshua and the children of Israel into the promised land, everything they needed, they *already* had it! From the time they sent the spies in (divine insight), to carrying out the extremely large fruit of the land (the power of execution), up until they went in to actually possess the land (the will to persevere). The power they needed was within them and not outside of themselves!

As a chosen Business owner by God, you have to first realize that no matter how much you study, how many schools you go to and no matter how many seminars you attend, everything you need is *within* you to activate the wealth God *said* He would give you.

Inner abilities are enhanced by Outside knowledge!

As you walk with me through this Spiritual Guide on Entrepreneurship from the Father, it is my sincere hope that you make this determination: **Stay on the journey!**

This is the best advice I can give you, based on my experience. I gave up too many times along the way and threw in the towel numerous times before I could see or receive my breakthroughs. And every time I gave up, I ended up at the same…….

CROSSROADS

You see, you will continue to meet the same juncture in your journey, if you don't do something different when you return to the same place. When you return, you have to take inventory and decide what needs to occur differently from times before. You need to determine why you are not seeing any progress.

We are going to deal with the many Crossroads in our Entrepreneurial journey. I have developed a blueprint that will help you determine how to press past those places of stagnation, defeat and the epidemic of throwing in the towel before seeing success!

Follow me, take some good notes, and most of all, get ready to start seeing the results in your business you desire. As you take in these nuggets of wisdom, and apply them, you are sure to start seeing your true purpose in business come forth. The original intention you set out in business will manifest as you apply these principles.

But then, you'd have to remember your first intention. Which brings me to the question: "Why did you go into business? What inspired you to step outside the box? What drove your passion to pursue your business?

These are tidbits to munch on as we take our visit to the many Crossroads which occur in business.

Keep munching…..

We're on a journey!

Chapter 1:
STICK TO THE BLUEPRINT!

And the Lord answered me and said, Write the vision and make it plain upon tables, that he may run that reads it.
Habakkuk 2:2 (KJV)

In order to stick to your blueprint, you must have first **written** your blue print as the Lord instructs us to do in His word. When there is no blueprint (vision) written, then there is nothing to guide or direct the course of your business. There is POWER in writing things down!

Where there is no prophetic vision, the people cast off restraint; but blessed is he who keeps the law. **Proverbs 29:18(ESV).**

This verse is what I consider a principle of the word of God. You must know as a business owner that the benefits of Biblical principles are not beneficial to Believers *only*.

The Benefits of Biblical Principles...

Please allow me to ask you a question: What business owners do you, or have you followed? Have you looked at their failures or successes? What do you think their wins or loses are based on? Do you observe them doing any one thing on a consistent basis that yields them some type of success? Why did you chose to follow them? Would you consider this person or persons a mentor?

I want you to take a moment right now and write down at least 5 business owners you know. Make special note of things you notice they do well. After you do this, meet me back here so we can talk……

Well, I see you're back! That means you will reach beyond reading this book and obtain similar *successes* like those you admire in the business owners you follow.

The main reason that I had you stop and take note is because:
> 1. As a business owner, you *should* be watching someone, and watching them very closely.
> 2. You should be able to determine what they are doing to yield success, and desire to duplicate that same type of success.
> 3. You should be seeing some types of principles active in their business activities. If you do not, stop following them immediately!
> 4. You need to look at someone's business model and decide how you can duplicate their model, based on their success.
> 5. Remember: It's ok to model someone who experienced failures in business. But your take away from their failures should be how they went on to achieve success.

Some of the people whom I admire most in Business may not necessarily believe on my same spiritual plane. But after experiencing so many blunders in business, I have learned I should be modeling success, and not spiritual beliefs ***only***.

I am a firm believer in the word of God! Please never ever mistake my identity of what and whom I believe. But what I have learned after looking at many other religions' thought processes and ways of believing is that *most* are operating in Biblical principles, just rephrased.

Most, and I quote very strongly ***most*** principles are Biblically based and are derived from the Bible in some form or another. How would I know this? Because I have been a Bible teacher, reader, and believer for the *majority* of my life. So, when I see something quoted, or practiced, I immediately recognize its source and origin.

The problem for us Born again believers is that *we,* and yes, I said *we* are not practicing these belief systems for ourselves and putting them to work like the world has. Then we get angry and swear the world is prospering more than us. We continue to complain, "How can they be blessed when we are living right and doing right and can't get a breakthrough?"

We are in denial of God's blue print and the way He intended for us to access businesses and business systems!

Let's look at some marks in the blueprint we may have missed…..

Accessing the Wealth

A good person leaves an inheritance for their children's children, but a sinner's (Wicked) wealth is stored up for the righteous. **(Proverbs 13:22-NIV)**

We often times quote this verse so loosely, and most times it is not quoted in its entirety.

We cannot quote one part without quoting the other. The inheritance we are to leave our children cannot be left without obtaining part B of this verse. This would be understanding how to access the wealth of the sinner, which *is* stored up for the righteous.

Do you consider yourself righteous?

In the latter part of 2017, I had a transaction with someone who possessed wealth (An Asset) which was being transferred to me. This person proved to become extremely wicked in their demeanor, motives and nature towards me. This behavior began to bring a whole new light on this verse to me in its entirety.

The Lord began to speak to me concerning this transaction so vividly and He told me, "You want the wealth of the wicked, but you don't want to *deal* with the wicked."

Dealing with the wicked, and just **talking** about getting wealth from the wicked are two separate things! We are ok with this verse until it is actually time to deal with the wicked wonders of this world!

Here is what I learned through this experience and I need you to take away: If it is the wealth of the wicked you are trying to obtain, you are going to have to persevere past their wiles and evil deeds.

Contrary to popular belief, the wicked are not going to stop being wicked because you need something from them. As a matter of fact, they are going to go on being even more wicked because you need something from them. They know that you, with your 'righteous self', need something they have in **their** possession!

There may be times during your transactions of getting the wealth of the wicked that they may seem to be taunting you or even knit picking you based on your 'need'. But you have to remember that you getting what they have is all a part of the 'blueprint' of God. This includes dealing with some wicked wonders who do not believe exactly like you do, but yet they have the **'wealth'** you need!

You must also remember: Wealth does not come in the form of green dollars *only.*

Here is a revelation, or revealing I need you to understand: **Money is not wealth, it is the manifestation of wealth**. Money is a byproduct of what you already have, not **evidence** of what you have.

There *is* a difference.

Let's talk about Wealth….

First off, as a teacher, I must break down what wealth is to you so that you have a clear understanding of what it is you are trying to obtain.

When I define this word, the first definition that comes up for the meaning of wealth is money. It is also inclusive of valuable possessions, property or other riches.

But the definition of wealth which is befitting to this revelation from God is that wealth is an abundance or profusion of ***anything***, a plentiful amount. It goes on to tell me that wealth can be things which have a monetary or exchange value; it is the state of being rich; prosperity; affluence.

As you can see the progression of the meaning of wealth, you should be able to grasp the understanding that wealth cannot be isolated into money *only*. If you isolate wealth as only money, you are missing the opportunity to have an **abundance** of wealth! Not to mention you will continue in poverty, excluding prosperity and the acquirement of riches.

When you are wealthy, you have no lack or need for anything, because you have an overabundance of everything! When you are in God, and operating in the truth of ***Deuteronomy 8:18***, you have a keener sense of awareness that you do not have to chase *money*, because you have *wealth*!

The world has programmed our minds to believe if we don't have money, then we are not wealthy. So instead of pursuing plenteous of substance, we only pursue money. The error with this is that we miss opportunities to obtain and tap into the wealth and substance within our reach! Most of all, the wealth God has locked up inside of us we **do not** tap into it and exchange it for ***money/cash.***

Let's break wealth down a little bit further. This is so you can recognize the wealth that you *already* have.

If you have any of the following, consider yourself a wealthy person:
TV's
Cars
Furniture
Ideas for products or business
Intellect/Functioning Brain
A healthy body
Time
Clothes

I could list so many more, but I will stop here because I need you to see these basic things are signs of someone who is wealthy.

And guess what? Regardless of the dollar amount in your bank account, comparing yourself to someone who is wealthy does not mean you do not possess wealth. You may not be on the same financial plane as someone like Oprah Winfrey, but you *still* have wealth.

When you consider the assets I have listed, you can take any *one* of those items and exchange them for a dollar amount. If **dollars** make you happy.

Sounds like our definition of wealth right? You remember the definition which said, "All things that have a monetary or exchange value?" This means although these items may seem menial and not of significant value, they can *all* be exchanged to produce money, or something else of value.

So, here is where we re-train our thinking patterns and thought processes. You have to see yourself as a wealthy person if you possess anything that is on what I would like to call our 'wealth list'. The amount of value of your wealth can be determined by the exchange amount or dollar value given for what is on your wealth list.

I have just about everything on this list. How much I will get for what's on the list is based on what I decide to cash it in for at the highest monetary value.

Earlier in 2019, I resigned from a job I had been on for 8 months. While on this job, the wealth I was cashing in on was my healthy body, because it was a labor job.

This was a hard exchange for me, because at the time when I started this particular job, my body was not in shape to perform the tasks.

Every night, I would come home fatigued because my body had been brutalized from the work I was doing. I was not prepared to be moving around for an entire 8 hour shift.

Before I took the job, I had been working my business, which was primarily ran from home. This meant I was sitting down all day at my desk writing books or doing what was necessary to promote those books.

Your body is an asset which produces money. When you are in physical shape and good health, you can exchange your physical body for monetary value.

WEALTH.

If I had stuck to the Kingdom blueprint, I would not have been brutalizing my body for money. I would have continued cashing in on the wealth of my brain and intellect. Cashing in on this form of wealth (my physical body) was not the ordained plan of God for my life.

We must understand there is a system of this world and then there is ***God's system***. If we believe in God, and consider ourselves Joint Heirs with Christ, then the system of this world can never produce what God has for us. We can try and try, but when we do not do it GOD's way, which is the way He mapped out for us, then we continue to hit brick roads with failure upon failure.

Well, what is God's way? This is something you have to spend time in prayer and fasting to understand. You also have to know what's in your hands, and the wealth locked up inside of you. When you gain a true revelation of these two concepts, you will then understand God's blueprint for you in business and entrepreneurship.

God's Word:
The Ultimate Blueprint

The best blue print to build from is within the word of God. I will share several scriptures in a specific order that will help you obtain your ultimate blueprint from God. If you apply them in this particular order, you will see consistent and continual progress.

This does not mean you won't experience challenges along the way, detours or one way signs. But if you stick to the blueprint, then you *will* ultimately achieve the success God has for you by His design!

1. **<u>Seek God first</u>**: *Mathew 6:33*
    No matter what great idea you came up with or ideas given to you by someone else, it is imperative to understand God's plan for your life. If you seek Him first, you can avoid the circles you will run around that we entrepreneurs who are "spiritual" can find ourselves in. I have literally run in circles for the last about 20 years since the Lord has given me the vision. Mostly because I tried so many things along the way to go *around* what the Lord was telling me. I could have been so much further ahead so

many years ago if I had just submitted to GOD's blueprint. This scripture rings with profound truth if we seek God first, everything He has for us will be added in His timing!

2. **<u>Be inspired to create and produce wealth generating ideas:</u>** *Proverbs 8:12(KJV)*

The greatest ideas and wealth producing products come from God. Even if the person who produced it is not a "Believer" in the things of God. If someone produces something that gives people a better quality of life, and helps increase levels of productivity, that *has* to come from God.

Every book I have written thus far has been an inspiration from God to complete. I get such great reviews about how a particular book has blessed someone's life or how they took a different path after reading what *God* had given me! When these ideas come from God, nothing but wealth can be produced from them.

3. **<u>Get educated:</u>** *Hosea 4:6*

When God gave me the vision for Power to Wealth Enterprises, I knew it was larger than me, and even larger than my human capacity when God gave it to me.

I also knew I did not have a clue how to execute the vision nor where the money would come from to supply what was needed. I also knew the Lord told me He would give me a business which would fund my vision. The mistake I made was chasing after the ***money making*** business, and not the ***vision.***

In a quest to manifest my vision, I went to

community college and obtained my technical diploma as a Small Business Specialist. This was a catalyst from which my faith would build from. This was also a very solid foundation upon which I could gain the knowledge I needed to run this Fortune 500 Company the Lord had placed in my hands.

Get Educated and then watch your blueprint start to grow, crawl and soon have the legs it needs to walk on its own!

4. ***Obtain the world's knowledge:*** *Proverbs 1:7*

One mistake we 'spiritual' folks make is we think the world cannot teach us anything. We also **do not** see the value of what they bring to the table.

This has to be the worst mindset to have. They are achieving success, so why aren't they capable of teaching us *anything?*

Did you know you can receive as much business knowledge from a world agent as you can from a believer? I am in no way telling you *not* to receive business instructions from a Believer in the faith of Jesus Christ. But what happens when the person God ordained for you to obtain knowledge from is *not* a Believer?

My folly some years ago was when God sent a woman into my life who was to mentor and train me. I messed up because I started looking at what she was doing and saying, and I did not like her presentation or pursuit in business.

Was she off? No. Was I off? Yes.

I was off because I chose to look at her actions and lifestyle. I made judgements about her that had no merit on the information she brought to my table. Her information was designed to propel me to where God needed me to be. I was too busy looking at the mentor and not looking at the principles and wisdom she brought that were meant to bring my success.

Learn from the world, don't *become* the world. **(Romans 12:1)**

5. **_Write The Vision_**: *Habakkuk 2:2*

There is a reason the Lord instructs you to *write* your vision. This is so it can be retained in your memory and carried out at the appointed time.

Although it seems like a simple task, when you write on paper, it becomes etched into your memory bank: a place where it is not lost. It's not lost because as you continue along in your journey, you will find your self actually *doing* what you originally wrote down.

If you do not believe me, I dare you to write it down! When you go back to your vision, you will almost find humor in the fact that you are actually *doing* what you wrote down without even second guessing yourself.

6. **_Walk in Faith:_** *Hebrews 11:1*

If you are a believer in the Lord Jesus Christ, then you absolutely know and understand you will be walking by faith and not by sight. Everything you need to believe in is not going to be tangible *all* of the time.

There are going to be times in your Entrepreneurial journey you will not be able to see your way, completely. There will be times when you will have faith for income to come from a specific stream, and it's not flowing exactly as you anticipated. Those are the times you will have to seek God even the more and walk in the measure of faith He has given you.

This is why *Romans 12:3* tells us we are to think soberly according to the measure of faith God has given us. If we try to walk outside of our God ordained measure of faith, failure awaits us every time!

7. **<u>Do the Work:</u>** *James 2:26*

We have to realize there is work that involves seeing *any* vison/ministry/business come to pass. Without the work, our faith is just plain dead, being faith alone.

When we work our faith, we show God we want it as bad as we **say** we do. When we do nothing with our faith, we are also sending God a message: we can take or leave the vision He has given us.

There is something wrong with a Kingdom focused Entrepreneur who will not put some work behind their faith. We cannot think everything is going to fall down from the sky from the prayers we pray. Everything cannot be Supernaturally done, there must be some faith proven by action!

8. **<u>Allow Him to direct your path</u>**: *Psalm 37:23*

Whatever we do, we must allow God to direct, lead and guide us. Without His direction *everything* we do will fail.

We can save ourselves time, money and relationships by allowing God's word to direct our path. I can recall countless investments I have made where God was not leading me. If I had the money I invested into businesses which promised to yield such great increase, I could have promoted my OWN vision ten times over!

We have to allow God to show us what to do with our time, money and resources. When we allow Him to direct us, then we will never go wrong!

9. **_Receive mentoring & counsel_**: *Proverbs 11:14*

There is absolutely nothing wrong with learning and submitting to a mentor or business owner who has been where you are trying to go! It took me a long time to get to this place, but I have finally realized someone who is of higher monetary status and influence can teach me *something*

The worst mistake you can make in business is not seeking out a mentor. I must add: a mentor does not necessarily mean this is someone you will be up close and personal with. You may meet them once or twice, and then decide to follow them on social media, their website or perhaps their blog. The point I am making is someone has been where you are trying to go and they can show you the best way to get there without all the bumps and bruises along the way.

10. **_Allow Him to grant you right connections_**: *The Book of Ruth*

Right connections can either make or break your business on so many levels. Even at certain junctures of your business, right connections can mean everything for the progress you desire to make.

Whenever you decide to partner with someone,

understand fully what they bring to your table, and what they bring is beneficial to **you**!

As we explore the scripture here, we can see Ruth being connected to Naomi meant more than where Ruth was at that current moment. This connection alone would make Ruth a star in the lineage of so many Bible Greats! This is why who you are connected to means more than just what you are doing in the here and the now. When you decide to connect to someone for business purposes, ask yourself these questions:

Will this person enhance my brand?

What exactly are they bringing to my table?

Do we share the same business beliefs?

What success have they experienced in business?

Can this success be duplicated in my company?

Will this person damage my reputation?

Do they operate in integrity?

These are just a few of the questions you can ask yourself so you can best determine how to move forward with this person or their company. If they cannot enhance your vision, then they ultimately will hinder or darken your vision and it may take you years to recover from the damage done!

The key here is to seek God first before you go out to lunch, entertain any conference calls or sign any contracts.

11. ***Allow Wisdom to be your guide:*** *Proverbs 4:6-7*

When wisdom is suggested to be a guide, for some it can be like talking a foreign language.

Wisdom is simply the best application of knowledge obtained. When you have the best of knowledge obtained, and you do not apply it well, then you are destined for failure on every twist and turn your journey will take.

I have learned from so many years of being in and out of my business that I cannot keep approaching the same issues the same way. If you continue to fail at what you are doing, then you are not applying your knowledge well. **This** is Wisdom.

The best example of this is for those who desire to be in business full time, and want to give up their 9-5. I can give you so many tips here because I have left jobs on the high end of the pay scale and also on the low end. But what I *can* tell you is whatever you decide, you need to stick to your plan and do not waiver back and forth with everything that comes your way. Just because it *sounds* great, does not mean it's a good fit for you and *your* vision. But then you'd have to know what your vision *is* before you can know what *is* or is *not* a good fit.

If you are going to be in business full time, set up a daily/weekly schedule and stick to it. Find a consistent source of income that will pay your bills, or secure a savings that will pay your monthly bills for at least 12-18 months while you build consistent cash flow from your business. The last thing you want to be concerned with is being evicted or your car being repossessed.

If you have not secured a savings, find you some consistent **income!** Notice that I did not say, "job, or part time job." When you find *income*, you are not locked into a schedule and you can remain flexible to working your business and finding your business flow. When you find a part time job, then you are not in full control of your time and you won't have the freedom necessary to develop and chart the course of your destiny!

12. _Follow through with Instructions:_ *Proverbs 8:33*

As you read this book, this will be a good set of instructions from God. Not only that, but I am sure as you take your journey, God will give you some instructions along the way.

Follow and do what God tells you to, exactly how He tells you to do it. And if by chance you are sitting under a mentor and they give you instructions, and their success has been proven, listen, and follow through. Everything God sends to you is to bless you and give you His Expected end! **(Jeremiah 29:11)**

13. **_Disconnect from Dream Killers_**: *Genesis 37*

The 37th Chapter of Genesis gives us vivid detail of the calamity of dream killers! Joseph had a very clear dream where God showed him he would be elevated. But the piece Joseph missed was the process he would have to endure by telling his dreams to those who would try and snatch it away.

Here is how you can tell if someone is a dream killer:

How **do they respond when you tell them your dreams, hopes and aspirations?** Do they lend support, directing you to good resources? Or do they frown, tense up and look at you as if you are stone cold crazy for having a dream? Take inventory when you tell a friend or family member your dreams.

Do they start talking negative after you share your dream? Are they telling you all the reasons why it won't work? Are they full of stories about the failures of others who did not make it pursuing the same dream as yours? Do they speak so much negative that you want to go and hide under a rock regretting you shared your dream with them? Remember: words are life or death; this is the power of the tongue! **(Proverbs 18:21)**

14. **_Protect what God has given you:_** *Proverbs 4:13*

I always compare businesses or business ventures to a newborn baby. It's figurative, but it helps you understand the seriousness of what you are giving birth to.

Your business, product or service is like a new born baby. If you are a parent, I am sure you can remember holding your new born baby in your hands and all the thoughts that went running through your mind at that moment.

The love. The Fear. The hopes. The desires to see your child succeed at life. These are all the same emotions running through us when we start a new business; we process them on the same level as a new born child.

We have to protect our new business as if our life depends on it. Just like a newborn baby can die of S.I.D.S., without protection your business will die in the first 6-12 months. These are the crucial stages of our business and it must be protected.

We have to nourish, protect and feed it all the right foods. And we most certainly cannot abandon it during this crucial time period as well.

It was the fall of 2016 when I attended a prophetic conference. I did not go seeking a word from God concerning my business, but boy did the Lord know what I needed.

I was called out by this particular Apostle and she began to prophesy to me concerning my businesses, and she put special emphasis multiple **businesses**. At the end of her prophecy, she quoted verbatim ***Deuteronomy 8:18***, and that was probably when I lost it. (If you recall in the Introduction, I quoted this verse as the original scripture the Lord gave me for my business).

I immediately went into a deep travail and I knew at that moment my baby had been birthed from the spirit realm into the natural realm. This was when the Lord started dealing with me about coming off of my job and pursuing my business full time.

Here is where I show you the analogy of your business being like a baby, by the words the Lord spoke to me concerning my business. He told me I had just birthed a new baby into the world and I could not just abandon it by returning to my job. He continued to tell me I needed time to care for, nourish and feed my baby so it could grow and produce the *wealth* He had laid up for me!

This is what I mean by protecting what God has given you. Keep in mind I was not prepared to come off of my job *financially*, but God was prepared to take care of me, I just needed to follow ***His*** blueprint and protect the investment He made when he gave me the vision!

15. **<u>No matter how long it takes, wait on the vision:</u>** Habakkuk 2:3

Please know and understand the vision may not come into fruition all in the same days, months or years you originally embarked into it. But the Bible tells us in **Habakkuk 2:3,** if it tarries, wait on it!

You absolutely must practice the art of patience. Not only the art of patience, but the art of perfecting your craft while you wait on it to come to pass. Perfect your craft, make wise investments and also remember it *will* come to pass. Even if you did not put every aspect of God's blueprint in place, you can go back, start again and then *wait* on the vision to come to pass.

The Art of Patience. You can do it, wait on it!

Whew! That was a mighty hefty blue print the Lord has revealed to us! I have walked out every aspect of this blue print, and I am in my waiting period because I *know* the Lord has given me the **POWER** to get wealth.

I'm just waiting on it! 😊

Chapter 2:
THE RIGHT EQUIPMENT

As an Entrepreneur, you have to know God equipped you with everything you needed from the time you made your entrance into the world.

The reason we do not believe we have the right equipment is because of what the world has programmed us to believe. Belief systems can be hard to break down. But the all knowing God has given you what you needed when He placed you inside of your mother's womb! God did not create anything lacking, missing or broken!

Let's Take Inventory…

Being and becoming the best at what you do takes time, effort and know how. The God's honest truth is you do NOT have to go to "college" in order to become a multi-millionaire.

You see God's goal and intention for us is not to just survive at business, or maintain this Mom and Pop status for 20-30 years of our Entrepreneurial journey.

Remember when we defined wealth? Wealth goes beyond just surviving. Wealth takes us from surviving to being able to build orphanages, wells and whatever humanitarian efforts the Lord has placed in our hearts to do.

So, when I suggest that you take inventory, I want you to delve deep into what gifts, talents, resources and abilities you possess. I want you to consider what it is God placed inside of you, and then determine how far these resources will take you on your journey.

I also want you to consider that taking 'inventory' will provide insight into your skills and abilities. These skills and abilities are transferable and can go with you in *whatever* business you decide to pursue. Remember, we are de-programming from the world's standard of being, thinking and living.

Here are 3 Parts to your inventory we will explore: **Skills/Abilities, Talents & Gifts**. Please note: talents and gifts are not the same. We will also explore gifts found in the Bible and how these are not the same as talents.

So, here we go……

Skills

Skills are the abilities that come from one's knowledge, practice, and aptitude; to do something well. Skills are also known as a craft, trade, or job requiring special training in which a person has competence and experience.

As we understand skills first, it is important for you to take inventory of the skills you possess. First so you know what you possess when you develop your business plan. This helps you determine how far you can take the business, and when to hire someone because your skill set has run out. Your business will die when you don't realize you have exhausted your skillset.

Here are some examples of skills:

Leader/Leadership. People like to say they are a natural born leader, and this can be very true. But according to our definition of skill, one can absolutely be taught the skill set of leadership. Your skillset will be most effective when you take classes to identify your leadership style.

Problem Solving. When you possess this skill, you have the ability to solve issues that may arise. This is absolutely a plus when running a business because you can almost guarantee problems are going to arise. Whether it's dealing with customers, vendors, or contractors, you will need to diffuse issues that can potentially harm your brand.

Good Communication. This skill can make or break your company. If you possess this skill, or work on perfecting it, then you won't have broken channels across company lines. Your communication needs to be effective and make a strong impact. This is necessary for company growth.

Time Management. One who is a good manager of time can get a lot done in less time. The person who possesses this skill can do more in 5 minutes than someone not skilled has done all day. Being a wise manager of time is a key component all business owners should develop and nurture. Time is something that can never be recovered once lost.

Talents

Talents are a special natural ability or aptitude; a capacity for achievement or success.

Talents can go so far and spread so deep within us. Talents however can be refined and fine-tuned so that they are perfected for monetary gain. Let's look at some talents one can possess for further clarity.

Examples of Talents:

Writing. Writing can fall into so many categories because of the impact it can have. One can be a talented writer of poetry, novels, books, blogs, and so much more. This talent of writing can be used in many facets of business, and can be most useful when it comes to marketing.

Singing. Singing is such a wonderful talent because of the joy it can bring to any room. Someone can be feeling melancholy and all of a sudden, someone can start singing and change the whole mood of the room! A really talented singer can go deep into the emotions of a person bringing healing and restoration. Or good singing can mesmerize you into a place of no return.

Drawing. Drawing is a talent which can be a beautiful sight in the eye of the beholder. The stroke of the artist's hand can create illusions that captivate the onlooker, leaving them longing for more. The talent of drawing has become so diverse that the artist can use the natural movement of the hand or the technical strokes of the computer's mouse! Whichever the choice, the talent of drawing can enhance the beauty of any room!

Gifts

Gifts can be defined as: Something given voluntarily without payment in return; as to show favor toward someone, honor an occasion, or make a gesture of assistance; the act of giving. A gift can also be known as something bestowed on someone without any particular effort of the recipient or without being earned. A Special ability or capacity; natural endowment.

When someone is given a gift, they did not necessarily do what it took to receive the gift. It was some type of favor the giving party saw in the receiver, allowing them to be trusted with the gift.

We also know the word of God tells us the gifts and callings of God are without repentance. This means the person's actions may disqualify them of possessing the gits, but God allows them to possess it anyway! **(Romans 11:29)**

Let's talk very briefly about the gifts given by God we possess. ***I Corinthians 12*** tells us about the spiritual gifts of God, and how Paul does not want the believers in God to be misinformed or unlearned concerning them. He also goes on to say the gifts of God are for us to profit from. **(I Corinthians 12:7)**.

This ultimately tells us God gave us gifts for us to

benefit from, but let's set the proper tone. The gifts of God are for profit, not for manipulation. When we are charging for 'certain' spiritual gifts and prostituting them in certain ways, this is not the 'profit' the Father is talking about.

There are certain people who stand and work for God who have certain belief systems. After many years, my belief 'system' has not changed, and I do not foresee it changing!

Here's what I mean about my belief system…

Let's consider some of the terminology we took a look at a few spaces previously within this chapter. I defined skills, talents & gifts. I firmly believe one should be able to capitalize (make money) off of their skill and talent, but not necessarily from the 'gifts' of God. You may be able to use the gift of God within your talent or skillset, but you should not be solely capitalizing off of the gifts of God. There is a difference!

Let's look at examples here, because I am sure there is someone who has picked up this book and is ready to go toe to toe with me about what I just said. You may even believe you should be 'paid' for your prophetic word, or your gifts of faith, miracles, etc.

Let's use the ideology that one should be paid for their prophetic gift, and clear this up for once and for all.

DISCLAIMER This is my opinion, not

Bible.

You should **NOT** be paid for your prophetic word! If you are paid for it, what differentiates you from the psychic? I am not saying someone should not sow into you as the Lord leads them to do so. But when you *require* this, you equate yourself to a psychic.

If you are using your prophetic gift for profit, like the Bible tells us to do so, then you should be using it within the boundaries of one of your talents, or skillset. When you use it this way, it makes using your prophetic gift "spiritually legal."

Let me give you an example, because I do this with one of the services I offer within my Publishing company.

A service I offer to authors is what I call '***Book Birthing Sessions***.' During this session, we take inventory of where the author is in their process (**Skill**-Good Communication). Once we take inventory, we proceed to determine what their goals are for book completion (**Skill**-Decision Making). After completing their goals, we begin to pray (**Skill**-Planning).

After using these skills, the Lord then begins to release words of wisdom and knowledge to the author (**Gifts** of the Spirit). Once these divine words are received, then we proceed to determine what are the next best steps for the author to take for their goals (**Skill**-Time Management).

Do you see how I used my gift, within the boundaries of my skill set? Glorious, right?

Yes!

Glorious because I can rightfully charge for my time, my skill and my expertise to execute the author's original intention for their consultation.

I used prophecy as an example because I have seen it abused the most within the Kingdom of God. There are Kingdom Leaders who put a price tag on prophecy, and I am sure within their mind, they have made peace with doing so. I am sure in certain settings, this is ok. I just do not feel it is ok within *any* setting.

And again, I am sure someone will say, well you just sugar coated charging someone for a prophetic word during your 'Book Birthing Sessions.'

Nah, I don't think so. I do not think so because the majority of this session will be based on the skill set and talents I learned and perfected over my publishing career. So, I am safe within these boundaries using my 'gift' from God to profit.

Allow me to paint a clearer picture in order to drive this point home:

You're on your job, and you are a customer service Representative who works in the collections department. Your job is to answer calls all day taking payments and making arrangements for clients.

Crossroads

It seems as if every customer who calls in has the same sob story about why they cannot pay their account on time.

On a particular Monday morning, you receive a phone call from an older client who is expressing why she is not able to make her payment on time. You hear this same story all the time, but on this occasion, your gift of 'discerning of spirits' kicks in. Normally you don't share certain payment options on your routine calls, because certain options are only to be shared as last ditch efforts to bring accounts current. Your supervisor has strongly advised you to only use these measures upon your "best judgment."

But as you listen to Mrs. Buckley (the client) explain her dire straits of losing her husband's income (who recently passed away), you know she really does not have he ability to pay, and your gift of ministry (Romans 12:7) kicks in. You start sharing with her the options available to bring her account current.

This is the perfect example of using your 'gift' within a paid environment.

Skills Utilized:
- Good Communication
- Negotiation
- Conflict Resolution
- Decision Making

Talents Utilized:
- Critical Thinking
- Writing (To document the account)
- Decision Making

Gifts Utilized:
- Discerning of Spirits (Recognized the spiritual state of the client)
- Word of Knowledge (Advised client of payment options available)
- Word of Wisdom (Placed client on plan to save her account)

From this example, it is plain to see how you clearly profited from your 'gifts' as Paul explained we should. You were able to do so within boundaries that were safe, and no manipulation was needed to obtain money, because your paycheck provided the profit promised within the word of God!

I know I went to great lengths to prove my opinion, but it was necessary to do so. In order to access the 'wealth' the word of God claims we can have, we have to stay on the safe side of using the equipment God has given us that comes in the form of Skills, Talents & Gifts.

So many have utilized the 'gift' of God outside of these boundaries and have fallen prey to the spirit of Mammon. Instead of working for God, they are now working for money, then greed replaces good motives and intentions.

Your Inventory Works....

One thing we miss as Entrepreneurs is that our skills & talents are transferable. We should be transferring the skills & talents we used in the world into the Kingdom of God. If we fail to do so, we neglect to see the usefulness of our skills to promote the Kingdom of God. We further neglect to see the 'gifts' of God have been operating in our lives all along.

Here is where I challenge you to take inventory of your skills, talents and gifts, understanding the difference between them all. Once you do, just like the example above, I need you to see your skills being transferred into the day to day operations of your business.

Most Entrepreneurs are like me, and have found many challenges in locating a happy medium between these extremes. What I mean by this is we can be on one end of the spectrum or the other. We can be charging for what should be given freely, or ***not*** charging for what should have a price tag on it; all while being taken advantage of.

I have been taken advantage of because I have given of my gift freely, yet robbed of my time all in the same setting. This is why I had to learn to charge for my ***time***, and not my gift. I continue to learn this life lesson daily: A person can have all the money in the world and *never* be able to pay for the anointing or gift of God within me.

I am priceless and so is my gift!

As you travel on your road in Entrepreneurship, know this: God equipped you with everything you need for success and school is not always a necessity. In the age and time we live in with technology, you can learn just about anything you desire, and it does not take mounds of student loan debt to do so. You have to be focused on the task and goals at hand and be willing to do whatever it takes to push past obstacles, hurdles and detours in order to see it come to pass!

I am not telling anyone who desires to go out and get educated not to do so. I am strongly advising you to use wisdom when you do and don't go into debt doing so.

When I desired to venture out into business, I went and got educated because I was stepping into a territory I had no clue how to walk in. But I started out small, and I used my own personal resources to do so. I used the tuition reimbursement benefit on my job, income tax and bonuses to pay for it.

The mistake I made was attempting to educate myself beyond my technical diploma. I decided to pursue my Associate's Degree and took out a very small student loan to "finish school". I did not borrow more than $3,000 of debt, but I am still working until this day to pay the small balance off.

I am primarily advising you to use wisdom by utilizing low cost and free resources available to you. Use these resources to sharpen the skills, talents and abilities already within you to pursue your business dreams and desires!!

You've got the right equipment: pull it out, dust it off, sharpen your tools and move forward!

Chapter 3:
Flowing Streams

And a river went out of Eden to water the garden; and from thence it was parted, and became into four heads. The name of the first is Pison: that is it which compasses the whole land of Havilah, where there is gold. And the gold of that land is good: there is bdellium and the onyx stone. And the name of the second river is Gihon: the same is it that compasses the whole land of Ethiopia. And the same of the third river is Hiddekel: that is it which goes toward the east of Assyria. And the fourth river is Euphrates. And the Lord God took the man, and put him into the garden of Eden to dress it and to keep it.

(Genesis 2:10-15)

This is a very crucial part of the word of God and His Blueprint (The Bible). This should help us to understand how to work and operate as business owners. We should never depend on one stream of income in any given case of business or circumstance of life.

I use this example because I learned very early on in business that one stream of income alone can damage your whole business portfolio. If one stream dries up, where will your additional financial streams come from?

It was the year 2008 and I was operating my bakery with much joy. I was full of excitement because the orders were coming in on a steady basis, even before I left my full time Corporate America job. Due to the steadiness of orders, I was barely getting any sleep, working around the clock. I was literally working and staying up until 6:00 AM to complete orders and keep my customers happy!

I left my job in April with no real plan for success. This was a huge error! The only planning I had done was securing my finances to pay my bills with the small 401k and retirement plan I had accumulated. I had not secured any pre-orders, and I had not planned any additional streams of income. I was solely depending on the customer base I had accumulated up until that time. I did not even have a proper follow up system for customers in place, I was simply "Stepping out on faith."

It was due to this lack of planning that I found myself in June at a serious dead place in my business. I had some other ideas I was working on, but they were not solid enough to fill the gaps of the lacking income my bakery now had. Considering the change of the season, cake orders should have been rolling in, but they were not. It was the summer season, which meant I should have been racking in some major orders. Orders like graduation cakes, wedding cakes and any other sweet treat that came with the change of the season. Instead, I was watching a phone that was not ringing and I was wondering why?

I mean, don't they know I have the best cake and buttercream frosting on the market? Don't they know I decorate every cake with love, and you won't be disappointed when you bite down into my moist, fresh and creamy cake?

I had not planned for streams of income, and my **one** *river had dried up!*

Crossroads

All of this meant nothing! It meant nothing because I should have done some serious planning **before** I left my job. As I reflect back, I am now certain that I should have sought out a mentor to help me work through those financial crunches!

When you are a business owner, and even if you choose to work one business *only*, you will need to decide on how you will bring income in multiple ways into your business. And if you are an excellent multi-tasker like myself, you should consider multiple businesses you can run to keep your cash flow rolling!

Your business model should reflect multiple income streams as well as multiple collection mediums for processing your cash flow. It's dangerous when you don't have multiple collection mediums in place within your business.

If one bank goes out of business today, and decides to take *your* money with them, what will you do? If you read the fine print when you opened your account, you'd realize the bank has the freedom to move your money around as they see fit. Do you also realize *their* assets and *their* portfolio's value is based on the customers whose money they hold?

I'll let that sink in for a little while……

The same goes for the collection mediums you use. If you are using ChalPayUp to collect your online sales and transactions, and they decide a payment from a customer has to be frozen, *all* of your money can be locked up for an extended period of time!

Now, let's consider this is the only collection medium you are using. You have money and payments that will process for the remainder of the *same* week that will also be locked up.

The only explanation they will give is, "Oh we're sorry for the inconvenience."

But this courtesy "apology" will not make up for the bills which did not get paid due to this **temporary** hold.

What are your plans? Are you going to go crying to the merchant provider, or you don't have to worry because you can easily transfer your next invoices over to your next merchant processor?

My suggestions all relate back to the scripture I quoted at the beginning of the chapter suggesting you have *multiple* streams like those mentioned in **Genesis 2:10-15**. God purposely gave Adam multiple streams of water because he knew one stream may dry up, and another may become contaminated. This is why the 15th verse says God put Adam in the Garden to "dress and keep it".

A major responsibility!!

I get grieved when people lose their job and it was the *only* source of income they had. I am mostly grieved because they either did not understand or were not taught the importance of multiple streams of income. I am not talking about a 2nd job, I am talking about *income*!

Crossroads

I gave some very wise advice to a young man I had the pleasure of briefly mentoring on a job I was leaving, but training him to fill my position. The advice I gave him was to look for *income* and not a job. If you look for income, you don't have to worry about losing a *job*.

Food for thought.

Here's Your Challenge…..

I challenge you to do the following:
1. Change the scope of your business
2. Consider additional income streams through multiple businesses

When you change the scope of your business, you are now looking for multiple ways for income to come in. This would be from products and or services as well as your income collection mediums.

As I coach authors through my Company, **IBG Publications, LLC** or my online Community, the **IBG Writers Group**, I give a consistent message to turn your book into multiple streams of income. I call this the, *"Think outside the Book"* approach. You absolutely never want to depend on book sales, only!

Let's look at an Example of how you can change the scope of your business by looking for multiple income streams. I will use my bakery as the example since this was my initial failure in business.

At the time, I was selling several products in my bakery. It was over time that I learned how to develop more ways of making money, here's what I learned:

Original Products:

Cakes, Cookies, Cupcakes, Pies, etc., baked from home.

Selling Mediums:

Corporate Offices: These were places I sold my cakes during lunch hours, particularly on Friday (Paydays)

Restaurants. I had the potential to Contract with Restaurants. This would have brought a consistent weekly income. My products could then be placed in the hands of consumers on a daily basis, giving me exposure beyond my kitchen.

Food Truck. Investing in a food truck would have given me presence in places like carnivals, local and state festivals at times of the year when business may have slacked off. This would have also given me the ability to hire a staff, giving me economic exposure in my community.

Flea & Farmer's Markets. Having a consistent week day in a place like this would have increased my visibility and produced more customers for specialty orders. Flyers and pictures of my work could be on display, which helps for repeat and return customers.

As you can see, it is not hard to expand your distribution within one company, you just have to be prepared and ready to do so. You cannot remain close minded to what could become a chance to take your dreams to the next level!

This is the fulfillment of Challenge #1
Changing the scope of your business.

When you opt for Challenge #2, on this challenge, you have to consider: Are you ready to open an additional business, or take on anything else?

Things will become very challenging, so you have to be ready. If you don't have a plan or the man power, what started out as a great idea, or wealth producer can crush you in a single blow.

Here are some questions & points to consider before branching out into an additional income stream:

Have you ironed out your processes in your first business venture? If you do not have a strong and steady blueprint for your first business, you will certainly be shooting yourself in the foot to venture off into something else. You are just not ready! It is not to say you never will be, but you cannot execute *two* plans if you have not properly executed the first one.

I had to learn this lesson recently because I tried to take on more than one business at a time. I realized I did not have the first one ironed out properly. So, I found myself going back to the drawing board on business #1 so I could get it in order first, *then* take on something new.

It is not to say it's not possible, but you could be making a road bumpy that was meant to be a smooth ride.

How feasible will it be to take on additional streams? This has everything to do with entertaining the right income streams. Most times when we go into business, we pursue a product we have a strong passion for, sometimes not. Regardless of which business you took on, think about the next one in the sense of: What income will it produce? Will this venture phase out in a year or two, or is it *always* a need for this business? How much time will it take this income to become consistent? Is this something I am interested in, or does it just make money?

Here is where you can determine what *types* of businesses you want to operate. I have learned that even if you do not have a quote on quote *passion* for a particular business, you can still work that business. But please don't do it solely for the sake of *money* because then you will be dealing with the greed factor and innocent lives can be affected. You should have some desire for the business you choose, or at least an aligned focus for doing so.

Have you considered the man power needed and the budget to take care of additional staff? It goes without saying that being a solopreneur can only take you so far in business. If you decide to take on an additional business, you have to make plans to either take on employees, or out source some of the work needed to be done.

As of 2017, I came to terms with the fact that I could not perform *every* task in my business by myself. I stopped trying to learn every skill set & every idea, all while draining myself of the energy I can exert in doing what I do best. I spent months paying for software I planned to learn to use, but never did. If I had used wisdom, I would have realized I could have out sourced the same tasks for less money. I am truly satisfied with staying in my lane, developing the skills and talents God has given me, and realizing when I've reached my limit!

How much time will it really take to get my new stream off the ground, and will it drain my current stream to do so? This is a tough idea to process, especially if you decide to take on a stream you are passionate about. When taking on a new venture, we have to be realistic about what it takes to get it going. This includes: the resources, time and man power it will take. You also need to ask yourself, how long will this stream need to become strong on its own?

Never ever take on anything new that will drain the flow of a current stream, and consider outside resources for financing. If you have been good with your credit, consider outside funding, and allow it to operate on its own budget. If you do decide to use personal funds or funds from your current stream, make sure the new stream can repay it within 12-24 months' time. No more than that.

If this cannot be accomplished with comfort, then reconsider timing and if you are within the right window of transition.

Don't forget: there is always the faith factor. If this is something the Lord told you to do, you may not be able to see your way *completely*. This is when you allow God's wisdom to lead and guide you into all truth.

After all, He has the ***final*** say!

CHAPTER 4:
A SOLID PLAN

By failing to prepare, you are preparing to fail.
Benjamin Franklin

If you don't know where you're going, you'll end up some place else.
Yogi Berra

It goes without saying that a solid plan will go further in business than just shooting at the hip. If you're old enough, you will know what shooting at the hip means. And if by chance you're not, it's simply going about without a plan and figuring it out as you go along.

I cannot tell you how many things I ventured out to do without any real solid plan. And *everything* I tried, ended up just like Yogi Berra said, going nowhere at 1,000 miles per hour!

What is a plan, in it's simplest defined form? A ***plan*** is: A scheme or method of acting, doing, proceeding or the making of something developed in advance.

This simple definition lets me know when I plan, I

am considering in advance what I will do, and how I will get what I desire accomplished. People who don't plan do not have a specific destination, they are just taking a trip. Their trip includes smelling the roses, but they don't even know if the roses will be there when they show up. They have not considered the season, or time they plan to pass by for a whiff of the roses; they are just ***hoping*** the roses will be there when they arrive.

Don't be the person out on this type of trip. Without a plan, you are on a trip to nowhere **especially** if those around you don't have a plan either.

Write it down...

I absolutely love those entrepreneurs who do not think they should develop a *plan*, structure their business or *plan* for anything outside of making money.

If you cannot see yourself doing anything besides making money: KEEP YOUR DAY JOB!!

Entrepreneurs & business owners should be accomplishing a number of things, ***inclusive*** of making money. The beginning of a great plan is determining why you are going into business in the first place. Once you determine your *why*, it won't be hard for you to consider what you want to accomplish along with your money goals.

Here is a checklist of questions you need to answer before you develop a plan. Read and check each question off one by one. As you move forward you will be able to write and develop your plan.

Before the Plan Checklist:

1.) Why are you going into business?
2.) What are your personal goals before you launch your business? Separate your business goals from your personal goals; they are not the same.
3.) What is the ideal business for you to operate? Is your ideal business based on profits or impact?
4.) What lives do you plan to affect while in business and how?
5.) How do you plan to give back to the community where you will operate your business?
6.) Geographically, How far do you plan to expand your reach with your business? Do you have international goals, and if so, who will help you reach these goals?
7.) Who are the key people who will assist in getting your business off the ground? Have you approached them about assisting you?
8.) What location do you feel is best for you to open your business?
9.) Is your business a seasonal business? If so, what are your thoughts for compensating in slow seasons?
10.) What will be your short term goals? What will be your long term goals? How will you execute them, and who will assist you?

I believe these questions serve as a good

foundation upon which we can start developing our plan. Let's consider what the word of God tells us about our "plan".

As we quoted in Chapter 1 from **Habakkuk 2:2**: "And the Lord answered me and said, Write the vision and make it plain upon tables, that he may run that reads it."

Key word here: **WRITE**. Without a written vision, those who come on board with your vision have no compass. The Word of God *also* tells us that where there is no vision, the people perish (**Proverbs 29:18**). This passage of scripture in turn tells us the people will cast off restraint, and they will once again be without a guide.

Can you imagine??

Can you imagine working for a billion dollar corporation like Microsoft, and there was nothing written down when you became an employee? Can you imagine showing up for an interview, and when you arrived, the interviewer had no paperwork in front of them? Not even an iPad in this modern tech world we live in?

Can you just imagine they are doing what we said in the beginning of this chapter: Shooting at the hip?? Making up questions as they went along with no real structure or order?

Would *you* want to work for a company like this? I would say, "No, I would not!"

Because I am administratively strong and sound, I am looking for the structure and order. And if I do not see it, I am high tailing it out of there because this tells me the environment I would be working in.

The order and structure you see coming in the door of a company is a huge precursor of what you can expect your day to day work activity to be like. You know the old saying, "The first impression is a lasting impression?" This is true on so many levels. If you are not a strong planner, you had better get someone on your team who is!

Any respected company has a strong solid structure. You want to be a company who garners the respect of your colleagues and peers functioning on this level. Your company may not start off making a whole lot of profit, but with a strong plan in place, you are commanding larger profits to invade your bank account. And one day it will, because you set the tone for this to manifest.

By failing to prepare, you are preparing to fail.
Benjamin Franklin

When you allow the words of this former president of the US to resonate in your heart, mind and spirit, you will never accept failure!

Let's talk about the plan....
My original journey in business started out back in 2006 when I registered for the Small Business Specialist course at my local community college. I had

no clue what I was really getting myself into. Within the recent years, my business picture has slightly become clear. I say slightly clear because without sticking to a solid plan, your progress can be slow and stagnated.

Here is what I also missed after taking the small business course: My learning did not end with the technical degree I had earned. I needed to find some continuing education to tap into. Just as time has moved forward since 2006, 13 years later, it still continues to move. Times change, laws change, people change, business practices and methods change and so has the way we communicate and get our message across.

Let's not even talk about the fact that Social Media has been on the rise since then. In the year I obtained my degree, it was pretty much non-existent and not on the scale we know of today.

With that being said, as you develop your plan decide what medium you will use to educate yourself about the changing times. You will have to invest in your personal development as an Entrepreneur, and you need to find a source that you believe in and can trust. Without educating yourself, you will find yourself losing ground and not able to really gain traction in your line of work. Let's also consider you may not be able to reach your target audience.

The business plan I created in 2006 was a great place to start. But any business plan I develop may be similar, but not quite the same.

Let's take a look at the components of the business plan:

1) The Executive Summary
2) The Business Description
3) Market Analysis
4) Organization Management
5) Sales Strategy
6) Funding Requirements
7) Financial Projections
8) S.W.O.T. Analysis (Strengths, Weaknesses, Opportunities, Threats)
9) Advertising/Marketing Budget
10) Goal Segment
11) Mission/Vision Statement(s)
12) Phases of Product Development and a full List of company Products

These are the basic components of the business plan. You can always list each component of the plan according to priority. I recommend taking a closer look at each component prior to writing anything down so you can gain a clear understanding of how to develop each part.

I challenge you to do further research into each component so you will be able to determine how to properly plan in each area. Remember the business plan is just that: A Plan!

Step by Step Actions…
In order to see Success in every area we listed here,

you must take a step by step approach in order to execute the plan.

There are tools and so many resources out there which can assist you in goal setting, keeping track of what you have accomplished and most importantly, keeping track of the vision coming to pass.

You must take a realistic approach to making your plan work. This means taking a look at:

1) Your current schedule
2) Your Obligations (current & future)
3) Who can assist you in the plan
4) Financial needs to execute the plan

Once you consider the above, now you can start developing your timeline for your plan. Please take your timeline serious if you are planning to transition from your employer. Especially if you have bills and obligations to meet.

Here are some things you can put in order before your transition:

- ✓ Eliminate unnecessary bills
- ✓ Pay down debts
- ✓ Bring your cost of living as low as possible
- ✓ Do not take on any new obligations
- ✓ Consider a shared living space
- ✓ Contact those who can lend you support along the way and share your goals with them. This would be anyone who can lend financial support, moral support, prayer or

perhaps business resources.
- ✓ Determine how much you have in savings and how long it can sustain you before your business needs to pay you a salary. Keep in mind you will want to project this salary based on your current living conditions, not your previous salary!
- ✓ Don't share your plans with dream snatchers and killers.
- ✓ Find means of income, and not necessarily a PT job. I have to expound more here. This is for those who are not the faint at heart and who do not mind *sacrificing* for their vision. Finding income means you may have to do some gigs or odd jobs to help bring income into your household until your business becomes stable. You can make income that does not obligate you to a schedule, which in turn leaves freedom for you to work your plan!

These are all ways in which you can start to get your life ready to become the business owner you always dreamed of being.

Here is another way you can execute your plan- start with some simple timelines like:
- ✓ Develop a 90 day Plan
- ✓ Develop a 6 month plan
- ✓ Develop a 12 month plan
- ✓ Develop a 24 month plan
- ✓ Develop a 5 year plan.

If you are having a hard time understanding what

these plans should look like, there are all sorts of resources you can find online which can assist you with projections, especially financials. Although money should not be the *only* driving force behind your plans, it absolutely should be a *major* factor in your planning!

These are some great tools to put into your planning arsenal. There is no cookie cutter way to approach putting your plan together or even what it should look like. Ultimately, your plan should look feasible for you to achieve and should be tailor made according to the *vision* God has given you.

Some other options you can consider when executing your plan:
- ✓ Join business networking groups to help expand your brand
- ✓ Locate business resource centers in your area who assist entrepreneurs with planning. Local SBA's offer a lot of FREE resources.
- ✓ Find a like minded group where you can get support along the way. (There WILL be hard times and you may need a shoulder to cry on or listening ear from time to time)
- ✓ Find a business mentor who does not mind showing you the ropes in your particular field of interest. Keep in mind that a mentor does not have to be someone who you see on a consistent basis. You can have a business mentor whose books you are reading, whose podcast you listen to, or whose business you frequent on a regular

basis. The point is to find someone who you can learn and glean from, and possibly miss some bumps and bruises along the way.

Beloved, I wish above all things that you may prosper and be in health, even as your soul prospers. **(3 John 1:2)**

It is the intent of the Lord that we prosper and be in good health in every area of our lives. This includes in the realm of business and business endeavors.

I am a firm believer that prosperity begins with good, sound planning. Anything outside of this is failure waiting to happen, due to a lack of planning.

So…… Happy Planning!!

Chapter 5:
SUBMISSION TO THE PROCESS

Process.

This word is so hard for so many of us to follow. Mainly because of the society in which we now live.

When the invention of the electronic device called the microwave hit the scene in 1946, it literally took on an evolution that is crushing the mentality of our society.

How can you say that?

Well, I can say that because the microwave has caused us to have what I would call a "microwave mentality."

I want it quick and I want it now!

We do not want to wait for the processes that are necessary for us to have bountiful blessings that last a lifetime and throughout our lineage. We have to realize that anything that comes quick will not last, and if so, for how long?

The seasons of Process....
I am literally tired of myself sometimes. Mostly because I have (Without realizing it) taken on this

microwave mentality. I have wanted what God said I could have, but had not endured my life process. Thus leading me back to continual…..

CROSSROADS

When we look at our seasons of process, we have to consider, "What is God trying to work out of me? What does He desire to do with me? Who am I designed to reach? What bad habits are meant to die in my life? What spending habits do I need to break? What spending habits do I need to develop? What mentality should I take on? What curses in my bloodline need to be broken with me? Who am I supposed to show that it *can* be done?"

There may be so many things God desires to do in our process. We are so busy wanting the processing seasons of our lives to end, that we do not sit long enough to allow the process to take its course.

Here are some questions to consider when God has you in a processing season:

The Processing Checklist:
- ✓ What is He trying to teach me?
- ✓ What is the intended outcome for this season?
- ✓ What fruit am I supposed to eat?
- ✓ What does God want to change about me?
- ✓ Who am I supposed to be an example for?
- ✓ What do I need to conquer?
- ✓ What is the expected Victory?
- ✓ What will be evident at the end of this season that I cannot see right now?

✓ What choices should I make during this season that will affect the outcome of this season?

After you consider these questions, you can fully embrace the season and not find yourself rushing through it.

I can think of my current season and how I have been here before. But I keep considering, "Why do I keep returning to this same place?"

I am sure I keep returning because of my **choices**.

Choices have everything to do with being submitted to the process God desires to take us through. I kept returning because I made the wrong choices.

It took me about 2-3 months to come to grips with the fact that I kept making choices that had me retuning back to the same place both physically, mentally, and geographically. Perhaps a different location, but still getting the same results: **Stagnation.**

When we continue making **choices** that do not produce the results God desires for us, we come out with the same worthless results. When we make God's choices in business, they are based on the *15 Marks of the Kingdom Blueprint* found within this book.

Re-read "Stick to the Blueprint" from Chapter 1. When you *Stick to the Blueprint*, you realize there is a 'process' involved.

My Personal Choices…

What did I keep *choosing* wrong? I kept *choosing* to leave *stable* income *believing* God would send these astronomical financial increases. If I would be honest, I had not planned or positioned myself for such increase. I did not properly calculate my business income, with projections that made sense up against my current income, which should sustain me beyond the job.

Season of Process: Job Transition

I really should have taken a class or read a book about proper transition from a job to my business. But I figured I had enough faith and I didn't need those types of "instructions."

I had this poor belief system: I don't need to be *told* anything, I have it all together. I've got great ideas and concepts. God should just blow on it, and make it all come together, right?

Wrong!

God ideas, thoughts and *wishes* (alone) just do not cut it in the business world or the entrepreneurial zone. You have to have a plan, even in your transition process! You cannot think that you are going to jump from steady income to instable business income and expect it to produce like your job did. The only way this will happen is if you decide to do a bunch of side hustling or odd jobs to make up the difference of what you were once making on your job.

Now, I do not see anything wrong with this, but at some point, you have to have a solid *business* plan you are working daily! If you do not wake up breathing, seeing and *working* your vision, you may as well stay on your job.

But then you still have to decide at some point is your vision a priority over money? If you do not decide which is most important, then you will find yourself chasing *money*.

I have found myself on several occasions leaving places of employment, finding myself stuck without income and *always* struggling to make ends meet. I got tired of that and finally came to the conclusion that I was making the wrong choice at the **crossroad** and it was taking me on terrible detours! These detours *continued* to lead me back to the same place: Needing a job!!!

Ok, I hear you out there, "I am *tired* of working for someone else." You know how MANY times I sang that same tune? Yet I found myself *back* in the same position because I did not consider the checklist of the transition season.

Or possibly I did not consider building myself up prior to moving out on *faith?* I would venture to say yes. Let's not even mention that I should have worked on my credit prior to leaving a job as well. At least if I had good credit, I could use it to finance my business venture, right?

Maybe.

I say maybe because I am actually grateful I did not use credit to finance any of my previous business ventures. I would have ended up in more debt and I would *still* be trying to resurrect myself. I just was not ready!

Well, what do you mean? "Audrea, I thought you believed in yourself and *your* vision?"

Yes, I *do* but these visions, hopes and dreams did not necessarily align themselves with the destiny and purpose *God* intended for me to pursue *first*.

I can recall chasing after one of my business dreams, that I still believe God for. The dream is to own a successful and thriving bakery with customers rolling in and out all times of the day and night!

But……

I recall it was the year 2013 and I was working my bakery business. I was baking up my 'loving from the oven' at home, and selling it in local Flea Markets. I was doing pretty good for the area and location I was in. I knew with time and diligence, my income would remain steady and eventually it would increase!

If you are reading this book, then you already know I make the best desserts like cakes, pies, cookies, and cake pops that you could ever dream of! I create dynamite recipes and combinations I have yet to see on the mainstream bakery market.

The scripture in ***Jeremiah 29:11*** says, "For I know the plans I have for you", declares the Lord, "Plans to prosper you and not to harm you, to give you a hope and a future."

And then comes the prophetic word of the Lord to me through an unknown source….

"Woman of God. The Lord says to you that your ministry is to come first and to be your first priority. He says that you will be able to do the business ventures you desire to do, but only after you do the work of ministry the Lord has called you to!!

The instructions of the Lord for you is to shut down your business and pursue the ministry the Lord has for your life."

Imagine how I felt.

Angry.

Yes, I actually got angry at God. I had no income besides what I was making at the Flea Market, and the Lord wanted me to shut it down??

Not shortly after this prophetic word, I found myself in a stuck, frozen state. I was stuck because I did not see how 'ministry' would bring me income that would sustain me. I had no idea how to turn my ministry into money without traveling from church to church as an itinerant minister; something I did not desire to do. I absolutely did not know how to convert my 'ministry' into dollars.

Here's where I went wrong:

#1 I did not seek God for Part B to the Prophecy. The Bible says, "We know in part and we prophesy in part." This person prophesying to me did not have *all* the answers, God did. Instead of coming to Him for the answers, I got angry at the person who would give me the answers.

#2 Somehow in my anger, I ***forgot*** the vision for business the Lord initially gave me. **Deuteronomy 8:18** tells me that **HE** has given me the power to get wealth. I just needed to convert that **POWER** into wealth, not necessarily dollars. Huge Difference!

Here I am about six years later finally tapping into *all* the Lord was saying to me that year. Had I sought Him at that time, I could have been about six years without so much folly, ***crossroads*** and detours which crisscrossed so many times! I could have tapped into my success which only comes from and through God!

I have done so many things since then, but I am *now* tapping into the wealth God had for me *through* my ministry. While I have been tapping into my wealth for the past 6 years, I could have continued working a PT job. This job would have produced consistent income and eliminated the heartache I have endured over this period of time. *This* would have given me the freedom to continue building my business while eliminating the headache of paying bills, which by the way do not disappear because we are chasing out entrepreneurial dreams.

Season of Process: Financial Transition

Crossroads

Here is where we free spirits have the most trouble. The troubles we have are proper financial planning though our processes.

In 2008 I decided I was tired of my corporate job. I prayed and asked the Lord if I could quit and He gave me the release.

What I did *not* do in my financial transition was proper planning. Now, I had savings built up but I did not properly plan those finances. I *should* have used those finances to pay my car off, and I would still have the car at my disposal to this day. I should not have used the money to pay bills from month to month, but rather gotten that PT job I *now* realize I need. I needed it now and I needed it them.

At the time, I was depending on my bakery dream to take off, and initially, it did! But then came June, and everything in my bakery income dried up! I started making bad financial choices and I did not properly invest.

I also did not calculate my mother's death into the year of 2008. I did not properly invest the inheritance left to me as a result of her death. So, what did I continue to do? I continued to make **bad** investments. I got a huge lump sum of money that I should have invested into something that would *make* money.

Instead of wisely investing, I started *investing* into bakery equipment and trinkets that I found on sale and later ended up throwing out.

If I were listening to the wisdom that was crying out in the streets to me (**Proverbs 1:20**), I would have sought the advice of a financial planner instead of continuing into the same pattern: using large sums of money to pay bills. Doing this depletes your financial assets; if at some point the money is not replaced, eventually it will be gone!

Now, I have so much more wisdom than to take large sums of money and put them into vehicles that do not have the potential to produce increase for me. I now know how to decide what good investments are.

When you submit to the process, you will not continue in the same cycles. You will consider what you have learned, and determine what to do with what you have learned.

You will eliminate anxiousness and you will not rush into *every* business idea and venture that comes your way. You will pray, wait and know when the Lord is giving you the green light and when He is giving you a *definite* red light. I had so many RED lights, but yet mistook them for green lights!

As I consider the Lord instructing me to hold off on business and do ministry first, my income would come. If I had realized this, I would not have continued investing into business ventures which yielded no increase. After *all* the investing, I *still* returned to my ministry.

I am grateful for the transition and I admonish you

to find the final place the Lord would have you to settle as an Entrepreneur. I would certainly advise you from my experience to thoroughly seek God before venturing out into what should be certain, but becomes uncertain because of poor *choices*.

I had a clear word, but I did not allow my *process* to continue shaping me because of the desire to see instant success. Success does not come overnight, it comes through a *process* which must be endured until *success* finally comes.

Submit to your process, the Lord has many great blessings to release to you. Not *just* for you, your lineage and blood line depends on it.

Don't just leave a legacy of money, but leave a legacy of submission to God!

Chapter 6:
THE FINAL DESTINATION: SUCCESS

What do you look to accomplish in Business?

Audrea V Heard

In business trainings everywhere, the presenter always start you off with the question **why?** They continue their presentation by asking you the following questions:

Why did you go into business?
Why are you trying to reach people?
Why do you want to make money?
Why do you want to be successful?
So on and so forth…

Your **why** has to be a solid **why**. If it's not, then you will find yourself in the place of defeat on so many occasions. This makes me recall my "why" when I first got into the bakery business.

My *why* was because I wanted to provide enjoyment through my sweet treats. I also wanted to give back to my community. Through what means? I really was not sure because I could not see myself, at that time, doing more than providing *free* baked goods and doing community events like back to school giveaways and helping children go to school. Feeding people was what I planned to do best at that time.

Over time, my *why* has changed. It had to change because if I wanted *God* to be glorified in what I was doing in the marketplace. I needed to ensure **my** why lined up to **His** why.

As a Born-Again believer, my *why* did not align to His kingdom plan and purpose. For this reason, everything would come crashing down in failure because I was not operating in *His* plan and intention for my life.

Your success is only predicated upon God's original intention and design for your business. This is why we have walked through **God's Road map**, took a look at **His Kingdom Blueprint**, and then performed a ***Checklist*** to ensure we are submitting to *His* process. No success that is real and authentic comes outside of God.

Through writing this book, I have finally come to terms with what my success is. I have been a failure many times over because I did not realize my success was in God's original intention and design and not in money.

The battle with money…… Another book I will write soon.

God's original intention for His children in business is to obtain the success He has for the way He ordained. It may take some time to get there, but I can guarantee you that if you continue in your process, no matter how long it takes, you *will* gain the success He ordained!

This is why the word of God Declares for us: Seek ye first the kingdom of God, and His righteousness; and all these things shall be added unto you. **(Matthew 6:33)**

I often tarried in my success because I did not seek God *first*. I have been the victim of failure on so many occasions. Mostly because I was trying to do things in my *own* power and not in the power, direction and leading of God. Bringing me to continual……

CROSSROADS.

I joined a group on Social Media where a business mentor, who is a Born Again Believer sends out a download. This download is entitled: The 6 Figure Framework for Christian Female Coaches, (Coach Beverly Walthour).

Within this download, she shows you how to frame your day so you can transform your business into a 6 Figure business.

The main goal of the download I my opinion is: As a business owner you should *start* your day with God, and your very *first* business meeting of the day should be with God, your CEO. If you have not met with God, how do you plan to orchestrate your day? How will your time be spent if you do not have His guidance?

When I read this, It was a major slap in the face for me. I was *not* seeking Him at the top of my day, and if I did, it was not on a consistent basis. I had to repent. I was not seeking the one who gave me the ideas, thoughts and vision to start a business in the first place.

Working within your own power when you believe in God is a very dangerous thing! Working in your *own* power when GOD gave you the vision is even more dangerous.

Reading this download changed my whole thought process, not to mention the course of my day! And you know what has *never* failed? When I sought God at the top of my day, I accomplished so much more than when I just let my day "happen". We as God's Kingdom Agents who are in business cannot just allow the day to unfold without consulting God. He will lead, direct and guide us into all truth. **(John 16:13)**

Success does not just "happen"

If you are convinced that you are just going to *happen* upon success, then you are sadly mistaken. Success does not just creep up on you and say, "BAM, here I am, embrace me!"

Success most times is a calculated measure that happens to those who spent a lot of time in between the school of failure, and many seasons of preparation.

Sometimes success does not come until you have emptied your bank account out so many times you can't even count, investing into your vision. Success most times does not come until you have been tried and tried in God's all consuming fire which is meant to burn up everything not like Him; even in business.

You see, wealth and success is not coming **through** *God* any other way. If you believe in over night successes, you are believing in a fairy tale that will never materialize. Success does not come outside of hard work. Let's not mention the fact that if you're not willing to pay some dues, your business will not be blessed from dreaming and wishing.

I *use* to be that person who ventured into business thinking I would defeat all the laws of business because I served the *All Powerful, All Knowing, All Consuming God!!*

We as Believers have some mixed up and backwards philosophies and ways of thinking! So much so that we are not willing to put in the *work* necessary to see our dreams and God's plan come to pass.

God's Formula for Success....
I am going to give you a very simple God inspired formula for success:

<u>God</u> + <u>God's Vision for your life</u> + <u>YOU</u> + <u>Planning</u> + <u>Strategy</u> = <u>SUCCESS</u>

This simple equation pretty much sums up this book. God's intention when He gave you the vision was for: **SUCCESS**. If you follow this formula, I promise you will see the plan and vision God has given you come to pass.

Your struggle will become eliminated when you stop trying to gain success outside of God. You will ***gain*** success if you follow the instructions given from this book such as:

1) Determine God's Blueprint for your life and Business
2) Learn and rehearse what true wealth is so you do not get caught in the 'money trap'
3) Take your inventory: Discover your skills, talents and abilities
4) Discover your flowing streams: Income, knowledge, understanding and resources
5) Discover the two challenges I gave in Chapter 3.
6) Develop a solid plan. Complete the Before & After Checklist in Chapter 4 & draw your timelines.
7) Submit to your process and do not rush it. Complete the Processing Checklist.
8) Submit to the proper transition from employment to Entrepreneurship. Do not rush this process either.
9) WALK INTO YOUR SUCCESS!!!

This road map the Lord has given me, I am going to test it out myself, or at least the parts I have not yet completed. I want the success that *only* comes from God, and it *only* come from seeking Him First!

As you put this book down, I want you to be honest with yourself and where you are in your Entrepreneurial Journey. No matter where you see yourself within the pages of this book, God's success awaits you!

Reach out and grab it, His success awaits you. All you have to do is seek His face, read His word and submit to your process.

Reach for GOD'S SUCCESS, not the success that will end in failure after failure.

Do as God instructed in **Isaiah 54:2**: Enlarge the place of your tent, stretch your tent curtains wide, and do not hold back; lengthen your cords, and strengthen your stakes.

May your tent be enlarged enough to receive *all* God desires to release to you today. It's yours, go ahead and get it!

Last set of Instructions:
1. Don't continue coming to the same ***Crossroads*** and not apply the wisdom and knowledge you've gained.
2. Success is yours-Claim it and ***Cross*** over to it!!

And Remember: The **POWER** is in your hands. Make it Your Wealth!

ABOUT THE AUTHOR

Audrea V. Heard

is the CEO of Power to Wealth Enterprises, and the Chief Editor of I.B.G. Publications, LLC. Audrea answered the call on her life to preach the Gospel in the year 1998, and has been on FIRE for the Lord ever since. She is anointed by the Lord to set people free who are held captive by grief and depression stemming from the loss of a loved one.

She is a full-time minister and business owner.

Find Audrea and her books online:
www.ibgpublications.com/book-store
Follow Audrea on Social Media:
@IBGPublications

www.ingramcontent.com/pod-product-compliance
Lightning Source LLC
Chambersburg PA
CBHW030009190526
45157CB00014B/1715